Be True 2 You
A Spiritual Awakening
Women's Impact Book & Journal

Phase 1 and Phase 2

Mia D. Williams

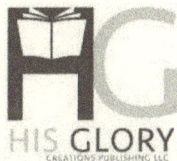

HG
HIS GLORY
CREATIONS PUBLISHING LLC

www.hisglorycreationspublishing.com

ISBN: 978-1-950861-30-9

Scripture references are used with permission from Zondervan via Biblegateway.com

Printed in the United States of America
10 9 8 7 6 5 4 3 2 1

Acknowledgements

I reverence my Lord and Savior Jesus Christ, my late father George Williams, late big sister Tonya Williams, my late grandmother Avery K. Grier, my mother LeBrenda Robinson & Jerry Robinson Jr., my brothers Myron Williams, Mario (Ty) Williams and Carolyn (Troy) Meadows, and Jyhonn Williams for the beneficial life lessons learned while still on this journey! Words cannot express how grateful and blessed I am to be a daughter, sister, auntie, and most importantly, a chosen vessel for the Kingdom Assignments! Mrs. Katara Townes, Ms. Diana Mungo, Mr. and Mrs. Cureton and Mr. Michael Medley who helped jump start this journey of mine.

Hebrews 12:1

(Stay the course no matter what)

~Mia D. Williams~

It was told that my parents would not be able to have anymore children! Look at God being very gracious and kind to bless them with a jewel from Kingdom!

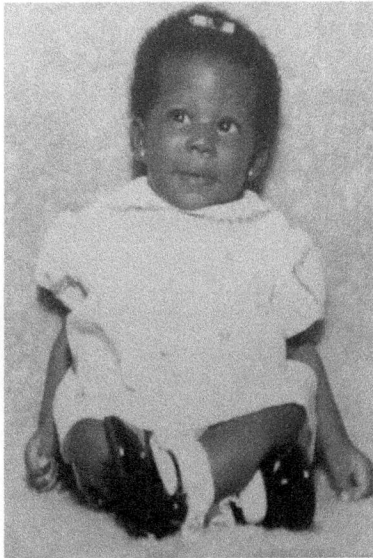

Be True 2 You: Phase 1

The life cycle of a butterfly truly is amazing. Butterflies as we know it have remarkable 4 life stages they must endure. As you read and journal through Phase 1 of Be True 2 You; you will see how this caterpillar ate through her tough shell to embrace the world as we know it! An earthly life begins with an natural birth. A spiritual life evolves from a spiritual birth. John 3:1-8

Table of Contents

Introduction

Grace & Peace,

This inspirational book and journal were birthed through and out of a once broken woman who desired more for herself but was unsure how to obtain it all in April of 2012! Hold on to your seats due to the daily entries you will read are all from a true and emotional place called life! All entries were never created by me (not made up) but were happening within me! I found my purpose, and I pray you will begin to be true 2 you! My name is Mia D. Williams, and it is so nice to meet you; now, let us get started on your journey to being more than conquerors and being true 2 you and those around you.

P.S. This is what I tell myself daily!
"What I speak, It Shall Manifest"!
~2020 Mia~

Entry #1   4/23/12

Healing?   12:00am

*Definition: Process of becoming sound or healthy again.

I do not know where to start when it comes to talking or writing about my now deceased father, the late George Williams? Why not, you may ask? It hurts every time anyone would say something about him at this time. It is like the pain in my stomach, along with the tightness in my throat, returns to me like it never left me. Our father gave us as a family security daily. Things were not always great, but who's family is? I will wait… but we were a whole family.

When our father passed, things kind of took a slight turn in everyone's life. With this new turn in my life, I began to place my feelings on the back burner and take on the role of my father for the family, if you will. During this process, I began to take care of my mother and brothers mentally, but I forgot about my own well-being. In my mind, I thought I had grieved already. Turns out that it was a total lie I told to myself. Again, Be True 2 You! Currently, my mind, body, and spirit were under attack for the next 5 years. And I almost lost my life over it BUT GOD!

My Observation:

*Questions: Have you ever lost someone extremely close to you? How did it make you feel inside? How did you obtain peace in your situation?

_____

_____

_____

_____

_____

_____

_____

Be True 2 You Response: For personal thoughts or key notes from the entry above.

_____

_____

_____

_____

_____

_____

_____

*Scripture: Jeremiah 17:14 NLT

Entry # 2   4/24/12

Marriage   12:40am

*Definition: Legally or formally a union of 2 people!

Now at this time of my life, not only did we witness our father transition. I myself was slowly going through a transition as well. 16 years of being in a relationship since high school; to the 8 years of marriage altogether; 24 years soon to be no more. Some would say things are coming to a bad end. I beg to differ that it was a deserved end!

We both were going down 2 different paths, and I could see it, but he could not! There were times I felt as if I was the bad guy due to the way he made me feel with words. I later realized it was years of built-up tension and unresolved issues that took root! He was the only man that I truly knew and gave my all; but things are changing.

*My Observation: This event made me feel less than at times. I did not trust men for a while. The only one I needed to trust was God for my whole life then; all will fall into place.

Write some experiences you may have had involving losing trust with someone. It does not have to be a situation involving a man. How did the situation make you feel as a woman?

_____

_____

_____

_____

_____

_____

_____

_____

_____

_____

_____

_____

_____

_____

_____

_____

_____

*Scripture: Jeremiah 29:11 NLT

Entry #3   4/25/12
Thoughts   10:00pm

*Definition: Idea or opinion produced suddenly in the mind by thinking.

I had a pow-wow with myself, and I realized that Mia had to think positive and carry herself accordingly. I started moving forward with my life mentally and slowly physically. Told myself that it would be a little hard to accept the emptiness of both father and husband, but I had to embrace it, encouraging myself to never allow Mia to deal with matters on her own. God had to be fully in control so that I would have complete victory! My thoughts were that true love (God's) had to overtake me in order to see clearly.

*My Observation: Do not allow your thoughts to run wild on you! You will end up where you are not supposed to be!

*Be True 2 You Response: In your own words, express a situation that you had to basically talk to yourself in a positive manner.

_____

_____

_____

_____

_____

_____

_____

_____

_____

_____

_____

_____

_____

_____

_____

_____

_____

_____

*Scripture: Isaiah 55:8-9 NLT

Entry # 4   12:30pm
Transition

*Definition: The process or a period of changing from one state or condition to another.

Moving from one place to another within the mind, body, and soul takes a lot out of you. My mind is still occupied with marital matters but feeling the singleness at the same time. Being torn between the 2 does not help anyone or anything. Change must occur for all transitions to be complete. I used to soak my pillow at night, dealing with every single one of my transitions that was hitting me left and right.

I prayed to the Lord to bring it back to my remembrance that I have been chosen by the kingdom to overcome each trial that I face! So, I went through all this, not looking back.

*My Observation: No matter what, keep moving forward! The only one who knows what is on the other side of through is the creator Himself! Trust the process....

*Be True 2 You Response: Can you relate to the above text? Feel free to write down your thoughts or an experience... that you had to keep moving forward.

_____

_____

_____

_____

_____

_____

_____

_____

_____

_____

_____

_____

_____

_____

_____

_____

_____

_____

*Scripture: Job 17: 9 NLT

Entry #5   5/9/12
Loneliness   11:00pm

*Definition: Sad that one has no friends or company.

What I felt during this time of my life!

- Feelings of hurt   Let down (towards God)
- Loss of security   Who would want or desire
                                me?
- Not being enough for   Will I be good enough?
  myself
- Trying to measure up   Expecting more but not
                                ready.
- Pain   What if?
- Feeling sorry towards me   Loss of touch (sexual and
                                senses)
- Abandoned   Overloading
- Spiritually heartbroken   Frustrated in all areas of life

Most days, I feel like I don't have a mate due to my yes for ministry. Also, the fear of anyone trying to get with me and finding out then; opting to bail because it would be too much for them. Telling myself that I am worthy did not sound convincing enough at times. So, what I found myself doing is overcompensating with people, places, and things! Whew... this is draining.

*My Observation: I do realize 100% that I am worth a whole lot more. My goals will never change about my personal and spiritual life going forward. Remaining true to me brings happiness and peace of mind! Be true 2 me no matter what is falling around me. I must remain standing to see what the end will be!

*Be True 2 You Response: Have you ever felt any of the emotions on the above list? Share yours below, and how did you overcome those feelings?

_____

_____

_____

_____

_____

_____

_____

_____

*Scripture: Deuteronomy 31:6 NLT

Entry # 6   5/12/12
Separation   8:30pm

*Definition: The action or state of moving or being moved apart.

While I am over here in my feelings about everything, I am now in a place where I know nothing about. I have mixed emotions about it all, I have moved into a new place, and it feels very strange. Why? Let us see to start with the fact that during high school, I only knew one man. Being with this man day in and day out was not healthy; but I loved it to my core! Nothing else mattered in my world except him. Yeah, I was crazy in love (Beyoncé) did not want anyone telling me otherwise.

Separation does not feel good at all since you have been with a person for so long. If I knew then what I know now; we both would have done things differently! The flip side of all this is that I no longer feel like I have (NO) voice at all. I am free, and living it feels great! Power and energy have been added to me to accomplish the mandate ahead of me!

*My Observation: Life is what we make it, and I chose to be great, strong and visible! We can choose to make it lovable, exciting, adventurous, and fun again. With God, of course…

*Be True 2 You Response: Have you ever experienced a separation? How did you overcome the emotions from said separation?

_____

_____

_____

_____

_____

_____

_____

_____

_____

_____

_____

_____

*Scripture: Romans 8: 31-39 NLT

Entry # 7   5/28/12
Down   7:07pm

*Definition: Toward or in a lower place or position, especially to or on the ground or another surface.

Went to visit my late Grandparent's grave and just talked while I stood there in disbelief. I miss them both, but I know they are pushing me from Heaven. My life has a purpose, and I pray I am fulfilling it with good habits and results for Christ's sake. Some areas of my life do not measure up when it comes to the natural, but who's life does? I will wait… most days I hope that they both can be present so I can give great wisdom and knowledge that I have learned along the way thus far!

I miss the jokes & conversations from my late big Mama Kathleen A. Grier and the understanding and security from my late father, George Williams! God knows best, and I could not agree more or would not dare argue it!

*My Observations: Never get in God's business because; you will never understand all of it! Just go with the flow of nature and spirit. They both work hand in hand. No one can stop the workings of kingdom or the order it demands. Be True 2 You and make sure to enjoy your family to the fullest, even if you do not want to.

*Be True 2 You Response: Feel free to write down any thoughts you may have regarding this entry.

_____

_____

_____

_____

_____

_____

_____

_____

_____

_____

_____

_____

_____

*Scripture: 2 Chronicles 5:7

Entry # 8   6/3/12
Church   4:00pm

*Definition in Greek: "Ekklesia" public assembly or people assembled.

Service was awesome today! The mindset was quite different and open when it equated to the atmosphere at hand. I was immensely proud of myself for being focused on worship and praising God! I have a greater respect for those that are Pastors in what we call the ministry world. Stepping into many roles now; I understand things will come up just to make me stronger and wiser in my walk with Christ! In my time of reflecting on last week, I truly saw who Mia Williams is becoming during this journey.

What I went through was for me only at that time. I thank God for the testing of my faith and showing me that everyone has a person in their life that will push you or try to break you down.

*My Observation: Be careful who is teaching, guiding, and instructing you to your called place! They must line up with God's order!

*Be True 2 You Response: Write down any thoughts, feelings, or ideas that have come to mind.

_____

_____

_____

_____

_____

_____

_____

_____

_____

_____

_____

_____

_____

_____

_____

_____

_____

_____

_____

_____

_____

_____

*Scripture: 1Timothy 3:15 NLT

Entry # 9   6/3/12

Big Transition   11:44pm

*Definition: Process or period of changing from one state or condition to another.

It is now the end of my beginning to a new outlook on life, I am moving from my uncle's house to my very first apartment! How exciting… I can say I will miss the security that I had as for others being around me! Tired is not even the word I feel right now in my body, and this transition will prove to me that I can be on my own. Some said I was not ready and my ex-husband too, I had to make up in my mind that I will only put up with people, places, or things if I felt like it. God is on time with his blessings. Peace of mind is very essential to any transition in my life right now and forevermore! I am still moving forward with the aid of the Lord.

*My Observation: Change is good! Embrace it to the fullest!

*Be True 2 You Response: Feel free to express any thoughts or feelings you may have from this entry.

_____

_____

_____

_____

_____

_____

_____

_____

_____

_____

_____

_____

_____

_____

_____

_____

_____

_____

*Scripture: Jeremiah 29:11 NLT

Entry #10   6/8/12
Move   12:00am

*Definition: Go in a specified direction or manner; to change position.

Today I moved into my apartment and signed the lease! At this moment, I feel incredibly happy and overjoyed that God made a way for me, he has kept me through this whole stressful transition, but it had to be done! The joy of the Lord is my strength, and his strength brings me complete joy. I did it without anyone's help but trusting God's hands for my next step.

*My Observation: While you are moving in stealth mode; gain strength daily to keep going. Trust God in all you do for your life, stay lifted and encouraged.

*Be True 2 You Response: For personal thoughts or key notes from the entry above.

_____

_____

_____

_____

_____

_____

_____

_____

I pose a question… How are you moving?

_____

_____

_____

_____

_____

_____

_____

_____

_____

*Scripture: Matthew 17:20 NLT

Entry #11   6/10/12
New Start   10:00pm

*Definition: Cause something to happen. Begin or reckoned from a particular point in time or space.

I finally finished moving everything, and I was able to spend the night for the 1st time in my new apartment I researched and saved for! What a major milestone in my life that I have accomplished. Motivation and peaceful is how I would describe the first night. It means my mind was not racing all over the place; it was settled. At this moment in my life, I'm very proud of Mia because I've done all I was supposed to do concerning my freedom and success!

My love and understanding for God have grown deeper, while going through my divorce and separation, my Pastor at this moment in my life, Pastor Bryan N. Cropper of GPCFM, aided my fragile mental stages during this process. I then promised myself, my pastor, and mom that I would not drop the ball or fail them on this journey. I had to tell myself that this will work for me and I will be successful.

*My Observation: To know who you have in your corner or circle is very vital to your growth and staying abilities! I had to tell myself that God did not bring me this far to leave me or see me fail and the devil is a whole black lie! The race is not given to the swift nor the strong but to the one who endures to the very end!

*Be True 2 You Response: Feel free to write any personal thoughts you may feel regarding the people in your circle.

_____

_____

_____

_____

_____

_____

_____

_____

_____

_____

_____

_____

_____

*Scripture: 1 John 4:18 NLT

Entry # 12   6/11/12
Emotions and Thoughts   12:00pm

*Definition: A natural instinctive state of mind deriving from one's circumstances, mood, or relationships with others.

Wow-what a day! I had a training class at GPCFM, and my ex called my phone. You would think that with everything that has happened in my life concerning dad and divorce. My instructor told me to answer it, but I did not want to. I finally picked up the call, and he started to explain to me that he (my ex) thought about me and wanted to make sure I was alright. I said in my juicy mind, I know the heck he is not calling me to act like he cares now. My flesh did not want to hear his voice, my life has changed, and I am grateful to God for it all.

*My Observation: All things in my life work together, good, bad, and the ugly! The peace of the Lord is upon me; it is so wonderful. There will be hard trials to come, but I have the ID of Jesus Christ to gain my total access for my freedom to be in active status.

*Be True 2 You Response: For personal thoughts or key notes from the entry above.

_____

_____

_____

_____

_____

_____

_____

_____

_____

_____

_____

_____

_____

_____

_____

_____

_____

_____

_____

*Scripture: 1 Peter 1:13 NLT

Entry # 13   6/13/12
Discovery   10:20pm

*Definition: The action or process of discovering or being discovered.

Tonight, I discovered that I had to accept that I brought some things into the marriage that contributed to the downfall. I desired so much out of certain areas of my marriage that I spoke it out of my mouth a lot, and it was granted. This was not a good idea if I never consulted God first. This hurt me at times because I wished I knew things then versus what I know now. What I realized tonight is that it is amazing how I wanted what was not destined for me in the long run.

My mind is settling down in order to think clearly about things. There are times that I think to myself (being human) whether if my ex has hooked up with someone else or who is tried to talk to him. Oh yeah, he tried to say I was possessive about certain areas and crazy, to say the least, while going through my ministerial training/ counseling session, my Pastor Byran N. Cropper of GPCFM asked me if I or my ex had a change of heart would I reconsider working it out or reconcile with him. I said nothing, and I walked out of my training mad, saying I was done; I am now living with the fact that I have to be okay with living on my own and moving forward.

*My Observation: We may feel like we know everything at the beginning of any relationship. We must be certain of the decisions we make to better ourselves as a unit, any type of counseling that we seek will be beneficial to all involved.

*Be True 2 You Response: For personal thoughts or key notes from the entry above.

_____

_____

_____

_____

_____

_____

_____

_____

_____

*Scripture: Ecclesiastes 8:17 NLT

Entry # 14   6/14/12
Reflecting   12:17pm

*Definition: To think differently or carefully about.

Today I had another session with my pastor Byran N. Cropper of GenuinePraiz Christian Fellowship Ministries. We talked about my emotions and history that I could deal with now. Truly realizing how much time and energy I placed into this marriage/relationship to end the way it did, I acknowledge and accept my part in this dividing taking place. Pastor explained that it takes time and prayer to effectively get through the hurt and pain I feel inside that never comes out to heal. It was told to me through previous sessions that I created this relationship from start to now. How? By saying to the ex that he is my husband, and this is how it was going to be, trusting the spiritual guidance was not easy for me because; I still wanted to be right in everything and not wrong.

*My Observations: Through my time here within GPCFM, I have learned how to become effective and strong during my trials. Things are not always easy to hear or accept, but it will benefit my life moving forward.

*Be True 2 You Response: For personal thoughts or key notes from the entry above.

_____

_____

_____

_____

_____

_____

_____

_____

_____

_____

_____

_____

_____

_____

*Scripture: Psalms 119: 15-19

Entry # 15   6/15/12
Overload   1:00pm

*Definition: Load with too great a burden or cargo. Excessive amount.

Today I am on a major overload of what we call (physical) energy. I feel like I am getting ready to explode, I have been used to being with my ex for the past 18 years, and it is weird to me not to be. Those that know me understand that I am very finicky about my life as well as my needs. Period… Lately, thoughts of engaging in adventurous activities with the opposite sex; having company to entertain; physical touch, and plainly to be frank intimate moments!

I have nothing to be ashamed of or hide. I am trying to remain extraordinarily strong in this area because I have only been with my ex-husband for so long, and he was my first. After all that I have been through, I am glad that I have not lost the desire like most would after separation leading into the Big D= Divorce. Some days I feel like I am not worthy of another mate. At times, it does feel good to understand more about me and my cravings than to just push them away and hide! I must slow down and do for myself and enjoy life to the fullest! This is truly a big change for me because; I am used to taking care of everyone else.

*My Observation: My overload emerged from my own self while dissecting the totality of who I am as an individual in ministry and life. Taking time for myself is key to growing the right way. Pressure never begins with others first. It begins with you. My gosh, help me to remain calm!

*Be True 2 You Response: For personal thoughts or key notes from the entry above.

_____

_____

_____

_____

_____

_____

_____

_____

_____

_____

*Scripture: Luke 21:34 NLT

Entry # 16   7/4/12
4th of July

Currently in my life, I am grateful to see another 4th. I must say that it is vastly different from my past. It feels like I am a little alone but excited and restful for the most part. My life has truly gone through major changes within 5 months while seeing more possibilities for me. Yes, I do get the emotions of can I do this, or did I make the right decisions to be on my own, understanding that it is okay sometimes the enemy will try and play on our emotions and feelings to confuse us. Changing my mindset to line up with the kingdom provides me with security and peace! I will make it with God.

*My Observations: Embrace the change and transitions whether if you make them or not.

*Be True 2 You Response: For personal thoughts or key notes from the entry above.

_____

_____

_____

_____

_____

_____

_____

_____

_____

_____

_____

_____

_____

_____

_____

_____

_____

_____

*Scripture: Psalms 86: 4-14 NLT

Entry # 17   7/10/12
A New   3:15pm

*Definition: Once more; again. In a difficult or positive way.

Now, this is very weird to one because I have never been in this place before? It is what you may call new to my thought process! While in rest mode today, I felt very heavy, so I slept. Every aspect of my life began to crash down upon my head. You know my late father, marriage dissolving, my mother, and family; I never knew how much a human body could go through while dealing at the same time! WOW…. It is like I am inside a very deep pool, and I see the top, but I can never reach the top for air! No matter what I see in front of me, I must think positive in order to gain positive results. In 7 months, I will be known as a divorced woman and free at the same time. No, I never desired the "D" {divorce} at all, but this is the way this cookie crumbled.

*My Observation: I am moving forward and counting my blessings. This is not my pit to die in but my pit to take a break and pick up where I left off with my endeavors. God did not create me to quit or give up! My emotions are real, and I will carefully process them accordingly. Embrace to stay in the race!

*Be True 2 You Response: For personal thoughts or key notes
from the entry above.

_____

_____

_____

_____

_____

_____

_____

_____

_____

_____

_____

_____

_____

_____

*Scripture: Ephesians 2: 10 NLT

Entry # 18   7/11/12
What Else?   12:50pm

Being an analytical person/woman, it gets heavy after trying to maintain so much weight. I feel like I cannot seem to make ends meet more times than not. Helpless is not even the word to use for how my body, mind, and soul feels right now! I need physical and mental support like never. The power and authority that dwells on the inside of me has not been tapped into fully yet! A daily reminder for me is, "Mia don't forget who you are!" Trusting God and all will work out when I do not lean to my own understanding.

*My Observation: I have learned to not say or ask, "What else, God?" This brings on more issues to deal with at a rapid pace that I may not be equipped to deal with now.

*Be True 2 You Response: For personal thoughts or key notes from the entry above.

_____

_____

_____

_____

_____

_____

_____

_____

_____

_____

_____

_____

_____

_____

_____

_____

_____

_____

*Scripture: Philippians 2:14-16

Entry # 19   7/25/12
Thoughts and Emotions   9:20pm

- I think about my mother.
- Thinking about my brothers and their families
- I think about my position in life, church, job, home, environments, and peers.
- I think about my accountability to God.
- I am emotional when I am alone sometimes.
- Very emotional when others do not understand or believe me completely.
- Trying to figure out why people mix my passion for anger.
- I do not like the fact I can stand in front of someone and see what God shows me about them, but they have no idea and do not want to see themselves.
- Feels like going on no matter what!
- I will be successful in all I put my hands, mind, and body to!
- My life is still shifting as I write and speak.
- I love those that those I speak with get revelation of who they are truly in the kingdom without me telling them.

- I am healed, saved, delivered, set free, talented, soulful, giving, forgiving, grateful, thankful, honored, humbled, and amazed.

God is still on the throne, and He is watching over me as I enter safe sleep. Goodnight butterfly!

*Be True 2 You Response: Personal thoughts or key notes from the entry above.

_____

_____

_____

_____

_____

_____

_____

_____

_____

_____

_____

_____

_____

_____

Entry # 20   8/5/12
New You   11:35pm

Just a few more minutes and I will be 32 years young. I am emotional as well as empowered to even reach this milestone. Never thought I would be in my own place and working every day to move forward. My soon to be ex called and wanted to take me out for the last time. Granted I did not want to be in his presence at all. But my counselor convinced me to see what he could want or just listen and then go home; mind you we are not divorced yet, but we are in a separation process! This gathering will consist of me getting a meal, drink, and dessert for my pre-birthday outing. I figured what is wrong with allowing a friend that I have known for 18 years. I have accomplished a lot within 6 months. My thoughts are not the same since not being intimate with my soon to be ex-husband while on the outing for my birthday!

Legally I am still married to him, but the feelings are not there anymore. My hope for him is that he gains a successful life with someone, whomever he finds that will fit his standards or plans. Not for someone to find him, that is the way I did it, and it was wrong. I told myself that if I did not get married again that it will be okay. Tell me, who does not enjoy the company and a great time? My prayer is that I can be with someone who will allow me to do for us unconditionally. Well, it is getting late, and I am turning in for tonight. Goodnight butterfly!

*My Observation: Sometimes it is okay to be friends with your ex. Other times it is not that easy for some. I just want and desire someone to reciprocate the amount of love and passion I give out to them. Of course, this person will have to go through the Father to get to me! Do not have time to end up in the ER over stressful situations that I or someone else caused. Be True 2 You!

*Be True 2 You Response: For personal thoughts or key notes from the entry above.

_____

_____

_____

_____

_____

_____

_____

*Scripture: Philippians 2:13

Entry #21   8/6/12
My Born Date   4:00pm

I woke up around 1:35 P.M., ready for the day ahead. At this time, one of my ministry friends called to sing Happy Birthday to me! I started to think no one cared about me, feeling sensitive and emotionally thinking about all matters that were surrounding me today. I hopped in the shower, got dressed, put on make-up, heels and went to meet my husband (still at this time) to go on a small outing for the last time before becoming divorced.

We finished our gathering, and I was tired and sleepy. It was cool to kick it one last time. We both began to openly discuss our findings about each other, and unbeknownst to me, it was told to him (by his father) that I was playing games with his son. His father did not like that I was leaving his son. At this moment, my husband informed his father that he will move on truly when he sees or feels it is over. He is saying still that we aren't over concerning our marriage, now a lot of his family and friends are saying that I've cheated and I'm not in my right mind. Because I must be crazy for walking away from a man that has money and things going for him and myself. I realized at this moment that I really made the best decision with the help from God to start new!

Happy Birthday!

*Be True 2 You Response: For personal thoughts or key notes from the entry above.

_____

_____

_____

_____

_____

_____

_____

_____

_____

_____

_____

_____

_____

_____

Entry # 22   8/8/12
Next Day   12:30pm

Woke up this morning and my whole body, from my head to my toes were in complete pain. My reaction in writing my final letter to my husband was very draining and emotional. I know I cried for 3 hours; could not stop until I had no tears left to cry, a release of sadness was needed in order to accept my place in all this unfolding right before my eyes.

How I use to be, act and carry on sometimes as I look back; it informed me of my actions sown into the relationship from start to finish. Beginning to deal with the old (Mia) is key to any transition or change. Going into a new and different place in my mind was a little scary. I am emotionally spent and need to rest now… goodnight butterfly!

*Be True 2 You Response: For personal thoughts or key notes from the entry above.

Entry # 23   8/10/12
Release   11:00pm

*Definition: To allow or enable or escape from confinement or set free. Actions of releasing or being released.

Today is another day! Rose from my restful night in 3 days that I had not slept since my birthday! I am purging a lot, and it is not easy or fun. I have told myself that I am finished with crying about all this. This release is a part of my ministry to help others come through. Most of the time, I desire someone to help me through all this, but I must go through alone! MY sleep patterns have been off, and tightness around my heart. I recognize and acknowledge my part in all of this within my marriage.

This process for anyone will either make you stronger or break you down. Our lives will never be the same after all this transition! I pray that both our minds increase for the better. The reason for this statement is due to the known fact of both parties agreed that the marriage dissolved for good. Things now will be profoundly different but needed in order to grow effectively apart.

*My Observation: Being bound to a person, place, or thing does not stop there. We are more than conquerors through Jesus Christ who gives us the victory. Keep going through the process until it is finished.

*Be True 2 You Response: For personal thoughts or key notes from the entry above.

_____

_____

_____

_____

_____

_____

_____

_____

_____

_____

_____

_____

_____

*Scripture: Luke 4:17-19 NLT

Entry # 24   8/25/12
The Talk   11:40pm

*Definition: Speak in order to give information or express ideas or feelings; converse or communicate by spoken words.

Wow, I had a lot on my mind. I continued to lay in bed. While my eyes were closed, I heard God speak to me loud and clear. There was a surge of energy that flooded my body, and I waited for instructions—talking to God about my progression in ministry to do God's will. Realizing that life in general, personal life, relationships with others will all change, and they all will be affected soon enough. Life is always evolving right in front of me, and I dare not stop its process.

Took a trip to mother's; had a great talk with her, explained that I knew I was bad back in the day growing up. What I found out next kind of hurt me because I did not know to the fullest degree how much of a difficult child, I was for her. She explained that I was rebellious toward her and the things she tried to teach me most of the time growing up. Grateful for the lessons she thought I never obtained and knowing that our relationship/friendship and bond never changed despite what it looked like to others and each other. Turning in now for tonight!

*My Observation: No matter what happens in your life, always maintain your connections and relationships with those that are beneficial to your life in the long run. Life is too short to dismiss the one you love.

*Be True 2 You Response: For personal thoughts or key notes from the entry above.

_____

_____

_____

_____

_____

_____

_____

*Scripture: Philippians 4:6-7 NLT

Entry # 25   10/11/12
Major Mental Shift

*Definition: Mental relates to the mind. Shift is to move or cause to move from one place to another.

This day was not good at all. Why you ask? It marked the anniversary date for my husband and I; it feels heavy on me. Emotions that hit me out of nowhere surprised me a great deal. I began to get sick in my body along with my actions and speech. Find myself falling into a deep depression never tapped before! My then husband called that morning to say happy anniversary. I went to work, and it was a gloomy for me the rest of the day. To top it all off, I was told at my job that my hours were cut so bad I barely made enough to cover my new rent payment. Life as I knew it was spinning inside of a funnel, and I felt every twist and turn.

This reaction made me shut down and could not think straight at times. I began to pick myself up and proceed forward, realizing what does not kill me makes me stronger! I thank God at this turn in my natural and spiritual life because; he keeps me grounded. Things happen for a reason, and I am going with the flow of it all. Taking one day at a time is all I can do or worry about, taking into consideration that I have done everything possible to counseling, talks, and nothing worked for us. It all came back to my face that "I was the problem," and he is fine; my will is over, and God's will be in front.

Happy Final Anniversary!

*Be True 2 You Response: For personal thoughts or key notes from the entry above.

_____

_____

_____

_____

_____

_____

_____

_____

_____

_____

_____

_____

Entry # 26   12/31/12
It is Finished!   7:15pm

2012 has been a year to remember and possibly forget. My life after tonight will be totally different! It is like I knew this world that I created with someone for 18 years. Now it will be all over at the stroke of a pen and the judge saying case is closed with a certified stamp. Seeing now that I am in ministry, it pulls on you in a different way when you have said "YES" to God! God is keeping and guiding me in the right direction; So, I am paying attention for real, for real. My love for God has grown even more, and I will not allow anyone to come in between that!

A lot has changed within this journey called ministry. Amazed at how I deal and perform amid situations that use to get me off track bad! Continuing to line up with God while walking the yellow line while looking straight ahead! I have a total of 31 days until my divorce will be final. Wow: so many years together will come down to one day that will solidify the end of a thing with no hesitation.

*My Observation: Whether something works or not; you never stop evolving to be a bigger and better you for those watching and waiting on you! My success is not based on a single person other than my efforts and determination! God is my strength, strong tower, helper and provider. God first, and the rest will follow!

*Be True 2 You Response: For personal thoughts or key notes from the entry above.

_____

_____

_____

_____

_____

_____

_____

_____

_____

_____

_____

_____

_____

*Scripture: James 1:4 NLT

Phase 1 Review

- My last name was still Kirkpatrick in 2012!

- I experienced the pain of my father passing before I was to get married in 2003!

- Packed my bags and left my home and marriage in 2012!

- Moved in with my uncle and mom for 4 months!

- Moved into my new apartment!

- Went to the ER with my mom on March 18, 2012. Found out I had neck and back sprain from the silent killer of the majority of African Americans = STRESS!

- My birthday was a blindsided slap in the face while going through my separation and divorce!

- October 23, 2012, back in the ER with a profoundly serious infection, blood pressure was 180/160, and the doctor informed me that I was getting ready to have a stroke!

- Obama became the 44th President of the United States of America on November 6, 2012!

- Had to pawn my beautiful wedding bands to stay in my apartment. Being stubborn at this point!

- Christmas is here, and I only have a few more days until I am officially divorced and called single! WOW!

**Phase 1 almost took me out...

BUT GOD!!**

Spiritual Awakening: Phase 2
Get Ready, Set, Go!!!

Phase 2 is a process where we begin to witness the maneuvering abilities of the caterpillar from birth to eating, crawling and climbing throughout it's life. This transformation is special in its own way. Just as the caterpillar preps itself to incase within a shell of protection while change takes place. The same happens with a child in Kingdom will be placed in the wilderness for their own protection while the Lord himself will strip the old man in order to allow the new man to emerge and produce great results! Where there's no sign of struggle, no beauty can't be built within.

Table of Contents

Entry # 1   1/12/13
New Year   11:08pm

New year is here! I am feeling so good about it as well. Change is
present once again; it is like once you are done with one area,
here comes another ASAP! I did say that my 2013 was going to
be a great year for me! At this moment, I feel good for not going
off on those that think I did not or do not know what they said
about me. Yes, it is clear to me that those you thought you knew
or known would never speak heavy or dangerous things about
you concerning who I was married too.

My life is changing in a big way, but I am excited to embrace it,
New Year, New Me! Brothers are starting to holler at this brown-
skinned woman. It feels good to my emotions but not my spirit
right now. To know that you still have the attraction factor is
good. After going through so much pain, I did not feel or at least
thought I was attractive to or for anyone!

*Spiritual Awakening Response: For personal thoughts or key
notes from the entry above.

Entry # 2   1/22/13
Terrific Tuesday   11:30pm

Terrific Tuesday started off cold. Wanted to stay in bed all day, seeing that I felt like I was finally getting some rest after a stressful year I had. My body started shifting back and forth it did not feel completely right to me. Made a phone call to my Pastor Bryan N. Cropper to inform him that I was going to either stay home or attend our bible study. I was used to being fussed at due to my name having another title in front of it. Meaning that I am now a licensed minister, and many are looking at how I respond to everything.

I felt it was a test for myself and him. We both passed; shocked is what I felt. My emotions are all over the place, seeing that I am used to being alone with someone daily at night. It is just me now, and I have needs like any other person/human being in the natural and spiritual sense of it all. Many men hit on me, and I feel like it is too soon. I do know that when it comes down to me being with someone, he will have to love all of me!

*My Observation: Going from married to single is not an easy thing to do. It almost reminds you of the process of trying to learn how to walk all over again. God's time is not my time, and I have to be alright with it until my true change comes. Stay encouraged Mia.

*Spiritual Awakening Response: For personal thoughts or key notes from the entry above.

_____

_____

_____

_____

_____

_____

_____

_____

_____

_____

_____

_____

*Scripture: Job 14:14 NLT

Entry # 3   3/2/13
Hell's Fire   10:30pm

I am beyond shocked right now! It is more like I am (Jello) mad
as Hell's Fire! Never knew that hanging up on someone makes
you very mature. Not at all, says the Master of us all, things like
this must stop or it will unbelievably be bad moving forward.
Asking a question is a problem, it seems, these days. Who am I a
dumb <u>sheep</u>! No, I am a whole loaf of yummy bread that has a
huge burst of flavor. No one said that I was trying to be a
shepherd. That line to my ears has gotten old, to say the least. I
can see right through it all. My name has weight with or without a
title attached to it! My mother and father taught me growing up
early that I have always been a bright light to the world, and I am
somebody without telling me!

Growing up, parents told us to treat those in front of you the way
you want to be treated. God is showing me what and how I must
grow myself first then others when things are done to me! Does
not matter how upset you may be at the person now. Never hang
up on them. It could be the last time you hear their voice or keep
them from losing their minds or what have you! Nope, not about
me being tough; I just need answers that make sense or that gel!

*My Observation: God continues to show me what not to do and how to handle situations that will come my way of being a minister. Oh, but one thing for sure is that this vessel is not a fool or dumb by no means!

*Spiritual Awakening Response: For personal thoughts or key notes from the entry above.

_____

_____

_____

_____

_____

_____

_____

_____

_____

_____

_____

*Scripture: 1 Peter 1:7-9 NLT

Entry # 4   3/10/13
Forgiveness

Sun is as bright as ever! Birds are singing loud as can be. Things are always changing for me, and I am emotionally and physically drained. No tolerance for stupid stuff today! If I want to be happy, then I must decide to do so! I have forgiven, but all this lashing from the pulpit is not in any way effective for my growth as a minister.

Granted, I have done things to provoke parties involved; I just feel like I am the one going through something new and different in my life. At this moment, the attention should be about me getting things right with God and self. Becoming a great leader or pastor determines the training involved along the way! The proof is in the pudding, baby! Oh, and the famous lines most will use will be "I'm the leader and what say goes, and you're not the leader.

*My Observation: A human being, person, man, woman, by, or girl can only take but so much from another person. If you want someone to care, we must show that we care all the way around. Misery loves company. I refuse to be someone I am not! I love God created, and I know others do too.

*Spiritual Awakening Response: For personal thoughts or key notes from the entry above.

_____

_____

_____

_____

_____

_____

_____

_____

_____

_____

_____

_____

_____

_____

_____

*Scripture: 1 Corinthians 16:13 NLT

Entry # 5
Self-Love and Care

*This will be a fun activity for your physical and spiritual body!
Enjoy…

- Take a deep breath!
- Cultivate and Conversate with the Father!
- Clean out all clutter in every area of your life!
- Accomplish a goal!
- Get moving!
- What are you grateful for?
- Brain empty- Dump your feelings!

*Spiritual Awakening Response: For personal thoughts or key
notes in the entry above.

_____

_____

_____

_____

_____

Entry # 6   4/23/13

Lesson 1   5:45pm

*Definition: The amount of teaching given at one time; a period of learning or teaching.

Posted on Facebook; it blessed me!

Life lessons are what they are.... Just that! I've learned that no matter what, God is always in the midst of all situations standing by—understanding that I'm here for a divine purpose. I cannot or dare not hinder another's growth. 1 Corinthian 13; Love is... read it for yourself. This passage of scripture has changed how I handle and deal with my actions in how I affect them while on this journey. Revelation of his word is powerful, and it allows me to get things correct with me first, then, towards others.

_____

_____

_____

_____

_____

_____

_____

Entry # 7   4/28/13
Lesson 2   6:00pm

Today was a good day! Why? I had a chance to witness for the first time with my own eyes that I cannot and never will forget. I will not or shall not walk into a pulpit without my bible or sermon that was prepared for the people. My spirit was vexed for real. True I am not them and they are not me. If I did something like this, I would never hear the last of it from my leader! Thinking that no one in ministry would never forget their material when they knew they were coming to give a word to the people in advance? How does this happen? To sum it up, this day, I was in the ER most of the night and found out I had bad acid reflux.

*Spiritual Awakening Response: For personal thoughts or key notes from the entry above.

Entry # 8   5/5/13
Sunday, Sunday, Sunday!

It was an adventure, to say the least, when it comes to conducting or flowing in worship while being a sheep at the same time, Grateful yes, I was to the fact that the entire church was entrusted into my hands while the leader was away! I looked at it as a test of my growth in ministry after saying yes to my call! Honored to be standing in my Pastor's stead on this great day in history.

My life has changed, and there is nothing anyone can do to change that! God is great, and He will be praised! I will keep pushing to reach my purpose and plan that God has prepared for me. The <u>mantle</u> of God is great, and I dare not play with it like it is a toy. The change process is here again. Thankful for the chance to operate fully as a pastor in the Lord's church! Wow, it was invigorating to be in the flow of Jesus! Understanding that moving forward means or takes preparation, information, and application on my part!! Things just do not happen overnight. My journey has begun, or it began after I made up in my mind to do <u>HIS WILL</u> no longer mine!!

Taking care of all things that pertain to handling matters of a pastor is not easy at all! I prayed for this, and I never knew it would happen this way while dealing with or going through divorce, changing churches, and now working on a new location for GenuinePraiz Christian Fellowship Ministries east campus. I love you, Jesus!

*Spiritual Awakening Response: For personal thoughts or key notes from the entry above.

_____

_____

_____

_____

_____

_____

_____

_____

_____

_____

_____

_____

_____

_____

Entry # 9   5/8/13
Emotional   11:40pm

Very <u>Rough</u>
Very <u>Tough</u>
Very <u>Uncomfortable</u>
Very <u>Transparent</u>
Very <u>Raw</u>
Very <u>Emotional</u>

Type of Day!

*Spiritual Awakening Response: When you have a rough day, list some words that may describe how you are feeling. What are some things you may do to make yourself feel better during these times?

_____

_____

_____

_____

_____

_____

Entry # 10   5/10/13
Work Outs   11:15pm

*Definition: A session of vigorous physical exercises or training.

Been working out for a while now, and things are progressing. Eating right, as well as trying to sleep and calm my nerves, has been a challenge. It gets better after you have your morning prayer and small breakfast to start your day. Working out for 2 hours a day (never missing a day) and cool down walk around the neighborhood before turning into my apartment. The sudden drop in weight from my body and spirit! Feeling wonderful in my skin is attractive and powerful! And attractive thing! I had to buy all new clothes due to how much weight I lost from my divorce, church transition, and staying focused on the things of God! Yes, I was doing Mia, so I thought, but that was not necessary at all. God handles all things well, and I was so happy than I have ever been in a long time. When you lose your whole being over pleasing only one person or others all the time; it will drain and make you resentful.

I had to change that by getting healthy for Mia! It works when you prioritize your life and your days for greater! You begin to yield great results! My weight went from the 200s to 165, I was a size 10 again. Now that showed a lot of hard work on my part, as I stated earlier, that things do not happen overnight! I lost so much weight, my late sister, Tonya Williams, asked my brother Myron Williams if I was sick, too funny to me. I had muscle but not fat to pull away from my bones. Progress and workouts are not friends not until the end.

*Spiritual Awakening Response: How well are you working out your mind, body and soul to stay fit for kingdom?

_____

_____

_____

_____

_____

_____

_____

_____

_____

_____

Entry # 11   5/12/13
Boom, Boom, Boom!   6:55pm

I was in an accident this morning, and I am all shook up like Elvis says! Wow... it's like I almost can't win at times. Did I mention that it is also Mother's Day, and I do not feel okay at all, but I still pressed through? This is what I do. If I am not 100%, I still press on at 100%! That is draining and dangerous within itself.

Things are what they are, and I cannot change it or them. Some people just need to have their breaking or crying points just to get through to keep going. Some that are close to you will not allow it because; you are supposed to be tough, and you can handle it! I am not built like you, and I require different gear!

*Spiritual Awakening Response: For personal thoughts or key notes from the entry above.

_____

_____

_____

_____

Entry # 12 A   6/16/13
Father's Day

Father's Day was different this year! I was asked by my Pastor, Byran N. Cropper, to speak on this day! I was like, for real, are you sure because; I am still healing from it all? It was a bittersweet moment seeing that my father had been gone for 10 years, but I felt like it was last week for me! My mother, LeBrenda S. Robinson, came to hear her only daughter bring the word of God on this special day. She knew it would be hard for me, but I would get through it. It was a surprise she never told me she was coming with my nieces. I was so grateful God gave me grace and strength to finish with a powerful word.

*Bonus: Only God uproots what is not needed for our growth!

*Spiritual Awakening Response: What are some things that God has uprooted from your life that caused you pain but real growth?

Entry # 12 B   6/20/13
Communication

All I can say is that within this meeting, we are having right now.
The tension in the room was so thick that you could cut it like a
piece of moist lemon pound cake my mother would make!

Communication is key, and it solves a lot of problems as well as
headache & blood pressure issues! For all ministry obligations in
life, it is important to be very truthful to your core with the circle
or core group that aids you to go higher! This is on all levels,
realms, dimensions, valleys, mountains, rivers, etc. in Christ.

*Trust is risky but worth it all in God!

*Spiritual Awakening Response: Think back to a situation where
communication and trust was a missing part of the puzzle. How

did you solve the issue using communication and allowing
yourself to trust the process?

_____

_____

_____

_____

_____

_____

_____

_____

_____

_____

_____

_____

_____

_____

_____

_____

Entry #13   7/7/13
Calm   12:21pm

Today was very restful. I went out of town to get close to the water! Being calm with all the natural sounds around you, you can hear the faint convos across the sand; the waves crashing against the shore, and most importantly, God's voice speaking loud and clear. My instructions were to hide within his wings for refining and deconstruction of the old Mia to prep for the new Mia!

This transformation began early, and it is still very much so active in my life. I'm feeling emotional due to Aunt Flow was in town…. I know graphic but raw to my core!

*Tranquil rest is a must for everyone!

I read in my word in Mark 2:22 NLT. No one puts new wine into old wineskins. For the wine would burst the wineskins; the wine and the skins would both be lost. New wine calls for new wineskins.

*Spiritual Awakening Response: Think about the scripture from Mark 2:22 what does this mean to you? Have you ever been in a

situation where you had to discard the old for the new? List the
situation below.

_____

_____

_____

_____

_____

_____

_____

_____

_____

_____

_____

_____

_____

_____

_____

_____

Entry # 14   8/4/13
Lovely   12:00

1 year and 6 months! Being on my own is lovely. This tells me a lot that I can do anything I put my mind to. The only one who can stop me is me! This process is a beast, but I'm rocking with it until the wheels fall off! Getting back to my roots is essential to your growth in ministry as well as being whole.

All I can say is thank you, Lord, for how you have kept me through some dark times thus far! I know there are more to come, but I will remain steadfast to the end of my journey!

*Spiritual Awakening Response: Personal thoughts or key notes from the entry above

Entry # 15
Becoming a Pastor

What I have learned about becoming a pastor!

- <u>Monday:</u> Pray for the Pastor's Family
- <u>Tuesday:</u> Pray for wisdom in you Pastor.
- <u>Wednesday:</u> Pray Pastor's focus of Ministry.
- <u>Thursday:</u> Pray Pastor's health
- <u>Friday:</u> Pray for spiritual growth in Pastor's.
- <u>Saturday:</u> Pray for Pastor's purity
- <u>Sunday:</u> Pray God's anointing on your Pastor's.

*I am a prayer warrior and Intercessor with a keen eye (watchman)!

*Spiritual Awakening Response: Think about the title you have now, whether it is Pastor, Prophetess, Evangelist, Missionary,

Usher, etc. What are some of the things that you have learned since becoming who you were called to be? List them below.

_____

_____

_____

_____

_____

_____

_____

_____

_____

_____

_____

_____

_____

_____

_____

_____

Entry # 16   8/6/13
Birthday Love   11:45am

I am at work (daycare field), and it is my birthday yet again. To my surprise, I get a call to come to the front office. There was a package sent to my job on this day. This was unexpected, to say the least. It was sent by my soon to be ex-husband, the day before our court date for divorce. This is another phase, and that is new to me. I will get through it all with God! The Lord is my strength and redeemer in times of distress. Thanking God for every moment which is to teach me and grow me the right way.

It was a sweet gesture but kind of 8 years too late to spoil me with flowers. Asking for them throughout the years seems void. Gone through too much and not going back to what I use to know! I will not go back since the Lord changed my soul towards my next life and how I will be treated in the future!

*Spiritual Awakening Response: Personal thoughts or key notes from the entry above.

Entry # 17   8/10/13
Bittersweet   6:00pm

Part 1: Tonight will be the last night I stay in my apartment. Bittersweet is all I can say. Yes, I did it on my own with no help from anyone. It was 1 year and 6 months, but now it is time to save up for the house. No more games to be played by this chick. I have fallen in love with me again, and I am ready to explore it to the fullest! Realizing that I cannot get anything done by waiting on someone else to do it, for me, that will never work!

*Get my whole life!

Part 2 (9:30 P.M.): Just arrived home from a birthday gathering/dinner. It got a little heated between my ex-husband and me. I explained to him that I will not fuss with anyone on my birthday weekend! At this moment, my spouse (sits still) was asking why I would not give him another chance? He explained that he never realized that he hurt me, but he feels abandoned about the whole thing that is still in motion with the big 'D' filing. I told him that after this night, it was done. He would receive the papers soon, and I am not going back nor changing my mind.

Let me be clear here. Mia persuaded him not he for me. While growing in my walk with <u>God</u>, I have learned not to fall for the banana in the tailpipe cliché. My life has profoundly changed with amazement that I could still enjoy what it is.

*Change is inevitable. Go with the current and do not fight.

*Spiritual Awakening Response: For personal thoughts or keynotes from the entry above.

_____

_____

_____

_____

_____

_____

_____

_____

_____

_____

_____

Entry # 18   8/12/13
Reset   11:00pm

Hitting reset on my life is not easy at all. With everything happening all around me, it seems a bit too much! Things I could write at this moment I cannot because it is different. My life is an open book is what I always say to whomever I meet or encounter. God has truly made me to be a true example for all to witness the good, bad, and indifferent! Eyes and ears have not heard or seen what God is about to do with me or through me! Full steam ahead is what I hear from the kingdom doors. This is my 1st and final exam of life from God, and I must pass it!

It is a new season and a new day! All about my God is what I say and what he wants from me! My love for Christ is growing stronger even more to display to all. I will pursue what pleases God from this day forward! I can do all things through Christ who strengthens me! Back at 3510, where it all began!

*Spiritual Awakening Response: When was there a time in your life that you were in a "new season"? What did you do and what was the situation around your new season?

Entry #19   8/13/13

Words of Strength   12:00

- Difficulties come to develop us.
- Every storm is a <u>school.</u>
- Every trial is a <u>teacher.</u>
- Every experience is an <u>education.</u>
- I am victorious in all that I say and do and put my hands to!
- God is great and he leaves me speechless!
- Consistent with God; he is always consistent with me!
- I am healed, delivered, covered, rooted, grounded, humble, secure, trusting, affirmed, free, joyful, caring, and <u>FORGIVEN!</u>

*I love me so much that it feels refreshing!

*Spiritual Awakening Response: For personal thoughts or key notes from the entry above.

Entry # 20   8/17/13
Battling Mind and Spirit   1:30 pm

Eventful day on today! My mind and spirit are always in a battle state now. This is due to oh let's see; I just left my apartment that I achieved on my own. Then I am going through a divorce of my marriage. Did I mention that while going through all this, I said <u>YES</u> to my calling in ministry and kingdom? Wow… a lot. Some days I just feel like throwing the whole towel in!

I had to remember what the Lord told me. He said that the weight is going to be heavier or greater when anyone decides to carry and wear the <u>CROWN!</u> My speech and thinking have changed, which is a shocker to me! I must continue to encourage myself when spirits try to attach to me to bring me down. Every life experience is a lesson for the next person to teach the next willing soul for growth. Implementing change for the phases of ministry is crucial. Therefore, we must improve our stance every day to be counted among them that shall reign with him!

*Spiritual Awakening Response: For personal thoughts or key notes from the entry above.

Entry # 21-A   8/31/13

God's Protection

My happy self was on my way out for the weekend to do just that, weekend stuff! Out of nowhere, my car decided to just stop running completely. This all happened in the middle of the highway, mind you! Some type of turn of events. I was minding my own business. This situation could have been worse, but the Father above protected me to see that not one car driving towards me would be speeding to almost hit me! Thank God! One gentleman stopped to try and help me, but I could not get the gears to change at all. Yep, my whole car was locked down completely. This girl (me) would just get in a car and just drive without putting any fluids in it. My mind was not thinking about maintenance but to get it to point A to B each day!

There was a lady who stopped to ask me if I was okay. I told her yes that someone was coming already. She said, okay, have a good day and God bless you. My whole entire attitude changed at that moment from being chili pepper mad to cool whip cream. In that moment, God had to send someone to encourage me and keep me levelheaded to handle the situation with care. It is funny how the people you do not know end up being angels unaware! She had to put my energy back to God so I can give him glory for allowing the cars to move over as they saw me on the highway for my safety. God is so good!

*Remain calm. God's got it!

*Spiritual Awakening Response: We've all experienced God's protection. List a situation where you knew God had you protected.

_____

_____

_____

_____

_____

_____

_____

_____

_____

_____

_____

Entry # 21-B   9/13/13
Make It or Break It   12:13 pm

Right now, I am past the stages of being exhausted, tired, irate, overwhelmed, confused, frustrated, twisted, and in disbelief! Whew, the last 2 years has been a real doozy! It has been a major make or break me type of trials and tribulations! I just cannot even express any other feelings in detail anymore.

My body feels like what my spirit is lacking. No one understands me at all is how I feel now. Maybe that is a good thing sometimes; if they want to get to know me then, they must make the effort!

*Spiritual Awakening Response: For personal thoughts or key notes from the entry above.

Entry # 22   9/14/13
Divorced Woman   11:45pm

Who would have known that I would ever say the words out of my mouth that "I am a divorced woman"? No one says this one is coming at all! Thoughts ran through my mind of what is happening! Am I truly sitting in a courtroom about to finalize my divorce all alone with no aid from anyone? Yes, I raised my right hand on that stand while looking at a room filled with strangers who are about to go through the same motions as I.

My heart was racing, and I could not stop looking at my phone, just waiting to see if my other half were going to come through the door to finish the process of divorce together as adults! Nope... he was a NO SHOW!! I began to get angry at myself to think he would show up or even for him being a coward on trying to prove a point! The hard-brown gavel hit the desk, and he said it has been granted for my divorce, and I was all over the place with my emotions! When you have been the only one to show up for things and follow through it hurts. You lovingly share your virginity to the only one you loved; got married, bought our 1st house, tried having children but oh my body had complications, but I can still have children, the doctor said. 18 years of knowing the man, I fell in lust, an infatuation that turned into my type of love; not God's unconditional love that I later found out!

Being a very peculiar woman in Christ, it is not in my DNA to just put down something I only knew half my life and rush to go find it again with someone else! Timing is everything. I sit and think, will I ever get married again or will I just grow old alone? Being an overly sensitive but overly passionate stimulating woman, I miss and adore hugs and hands that hold with security and strength as well as understanding! A touch from the opposite is in true need, but I will be patient until <u>He</u> finds me the right way. Through God himself, he must ask then; my finger he shall have and to hold! Patience is a virtue!

*Spiritual Awakening Response: For personal thoughts or key notes from the entry above.

_____

_____

_____

_____

_____

_____

Entry # 23   9/15/13

Personal

Tonight, I am not feeling too great! So much going on around me right now. My life is sort of dim now. I cannot control any of my thoughts or emotions. We are not even going to say anything about the Father now. My body is truly going into shut down mode. I am forcing myself to keep pushing through these hard times! Personal things have been very twisted, tangled, and blind-sighted for me.

Things are starting to appear, and I feel so stupid for not opening my eyes to what was right in front of my face. I will not give myself a way to anyone the way I did for 17 years by being dumb with just self-love instead of God's love! I am greater, bigger, and stronger than all that! Sometimes being quiet is best!

*Spiritual Awakening Response: For personal thoughts or key notes from the entry above.

Entry # 24   9/24/13
True Colors   11:50

First night at Genuine Praiz leading intercessory prayer and
giving a word! I was disappointed in certain members because;
they would prove time and time again that they were who they
would show or display to the world when someone shows you
their TRUE COLORS or behavior believe it! We as a body are
always talking about never forsaking the assembly of the saints.
This was not anything different. I have a low tolerance for stupid
situations others try to pull you into. Don't come to me and say
you're all in and committed.

For what I see as well as others that do not even attend, we know
why you're here, and that is facts! Only for what you want or
what you can get is the goal at hand. Too funny to me that you
would think no one can see through all this mess. Secrets are not
secure but deadly to the person or place or thing it involves!

*Spiritual Awakening Response:

Entry # 25   10/3/13
One Day at a Time   8:31pm

As you begin the journey of what we call ministry. We begin to see why they say take it one day at a time. Never try to climb up to the top too soon before your time! Found myself doing things that I thought would help but it turns out it was not a help but a delay in my growth. I had to learn the hard way that if the leader did not request it to be done, do not do it yourself! I find that when a person tries too hard to make it ok for the other involved, it messes with how they must endure by God's standards for their own lives.

That is major to start something God didn't approve you of! The important thing to realize is that we as individuals shall never take matters into our own hands and get arrogant with knowing that we made something happen. Stay humble, follow instructions!

*Spiritual Awakening Response: For personal thoughts or key notes from the entry above.

Entry # 26

Losing Trust

10/7/13

11:40

Staring to lose trust in those around me right now!? Pressing my way to work was not an easy thing to do. Mentally drained is how I feel in the mind. Body is a whole different story. Shaky grounds are all around me now. Feeling as if others do not even realize that I am mentally and spiritually drained is defeating me! A get-away would be nice, but I cannot afford to right now. If I do not, I am going to explode with a lot of bad energy! Right now, my mind is saying I cannot handle any form of arguing or it will send me into a tangent. Can I just say that I am sensitive, irritated to the MAX!

Holding things in is what I do best until I cannot hold it any longer! It's bad when it finally comes out! The filing date for my divorce is October 17th, early in the morning. Time flies when you are not being productive! I need the release because it is time for it. Been through enough heartache and bondage, I placed upon myself. Just ill as a hornet, and I will sting someone if I could. Oh, I had a colonoscopy and had to check if I had precancerous cells on my cervix walls. Yep, something else to keep my mind going!

*Spiritual Awakening Response: For personal thoughts or key notes from the entry above.

_____

_____

_____

_____

_____

_____

_____

_____

_____

_____

_____

_____

_____

_____

_____

_____

Entry # 27   10/11/13

Determination   10:00

Woke up from a nice nap! The doctor called to inform me of my benign, precancerous cells on my cervix. I began to get overwhelmed with fear. A lot of things run in my family, but I am determined to not let them run through me or my family any longer! I will call those things which be not as though they were! Hallelujah! Romans 4:17 NLT. That is called will power and determination! If that was not enough, this day marks 10 years I am still legally married to my husband before divorce! Whew, a lot you say. My life has been a roller coaster since I was born, I think! The Devil keeps calling my bluff on this whole thing. The joke is on him because; I have never enjoyed games or jokes to be played upon me. Resting my eyes and my brain.

(Goodnight butterfly)

*Spiritual Awakening Response: How has having determination giving you the strength to overcome obstacles in your life?

Entry # 28

Do Over

How do I say this? Well, here it is!

When my redeemer, comforter, creator of all living things on this side of Earth has literally wiped, erased, pressed reset and given me a pass to <u>DO OVER</u> my life again from this point! I have an <u>Unwavering Mantle</u> upon me to activate and work on myself. It has been a tough road, but my journey has just begun! As I complete the great mission given solely to this vessel. God will be in the front leading my footsteps.

One thing mother used to tell me was, "Don't allow history to repeat itself ever!" (LeBrenda Robinson). What the Father ordered is what I will do! Letting go of infectious people, places, and things that stifle my purposes for Kingdom! I deal with it before it deals with me! (mindset)

*Spiritual Awakening Response: How many times have you fallen and had to "Do things over" again in life? How was the entire experience?

_____

_____

_____

_____

_____

_____

_____

_____

_____

_____

_____

_____

*Scripture: 2 Corinthians 11: 1-31

Entry # 29   1/30/14
I Win

Sarah Jakes Quote:

I <u>gave</u> too much of myself away and accepted much too little in return. You didn't hurt me. I hurt myself! (Powerful) Sarah Jakes

Holy Spirit is Speaking:

Tapping into our divine purpose-driven call on our own individual lives creates great opportunities to see <u>"YOU"</u> in a whole new light! God's Light. Mia

Independence and security within self is a great attribute to have and display to confirm and affirm that you can or have made it!

*No matter what comes or goes in my life...... I WIN!!!!

*Spiritual Awakening Response: For personal thoughts or key notes from the entry above.

Entry # 30   12/17/14
Last Entry

This is the last entry of volumes 1 & 2 of "Be True 2 You... A Spiritual Awakening... A Women's Journal and Book. A lot has gone into this, and now it is coming out for all to see and experience also to reflect upon their own lives of great change for greater! Many times, I started this process called writing it all out, but I would stop myself. We all know what that enemy is-- Fear! 9 years of blank pages in multiple notebooks for one brain to pour into while writing with one hand is a lot but worth every drop of sweat and tear shed. I pray that you can not only read about my happenings but also gain some strength for your current ones that arise! No one is the same but the goal at hand shall never change! An Apostle prophesied to me, and he told me that I have 3 books that will be published! I looked at him like, what, where? Then, he broke it down and said that the 1st book 1. My Life Story 2. Women's Motivational Pamphlet 3. Unknown.

He also stated that I would soon be coming into my own and a good season. I will not want for anything because of my faithfulness and determination for the things of God! Reaching a lot of women in big ways is a major part of my ministry. Who knew I would be completing my first book! It is almost

Christmas, and a new year is approaching! New beginnings from this point on! Moving forward, thinking wiser and stronger is the key! Volume 2 Coming soon.... Allow patience to have its perfect works!

*Spiritual Awakening Response: For personal thoughts or key notes from the entry above.

_____

_____

_____

_____

_____

_____

_____

_____

_____

_____

_____

_____

References

Bible Gateway/New International Version (NIV).
2011, Biblica, Inc

https://www.biblegateway.com/versions/New-International-Version-NIV-Bible/

His Glory Creations Publishing, LLC is an International Christian Book Publishing Company, which helps launch the creative works of new, aspiring and seasoned authors across the globe, through stories that are inspirational, empowering, life-changing or educational in nature, including poetry, journals, children's books, fiction and non-fiction works.

DESIRE TO KNOW MORE ABOUT HGCP?

Contact Information:

CEO/Founder: Felicia C. Lucas

www.hisglorycreationspublishing.com

Facebook: His Glory Creations Publishing

Email: hgcpublishingllc@gmail.com

Phone: 919-679-1706